Travel G____ To Granada

2023

Discover the Hidden Gems of Granada: Your Ultimate Travel Guide

Scott O. Cortes

Table Of Content

INTRODUCTION

GETTING TO KNOW GRANADA

HISTORY OF GRANADA

TOP SIGHTS AND ATTRACTIONS

HIDDEN GEMS

FOOD AND DRINK

OUTDOOR ACTIVITIES AND DAY TRIPS

BEACHES NEAR GRANADA

ACCOMMODATIONS

PRACTICAL INFORMATION

LANGUAGE AND COMMUNICATION

USEFUL PHRASES

SAFETY AND HEALTH

LOCAL CUSTOMS AND ETIQUETTE

CONCLUSION

INTRODUCTION

The legends of Andalusia, a region of southern Spain renowned for its stunning scenery, extensive history, and vibrant culture, had long captivated Anna. She had always fantasised about exploring the historic neighbourhoods of Granada, following in the footsteps of long-gone civilizations, and becoming engrossed in the entrancing charm of the city.

Anna felt she had to take advantage of the chance to visit Granada when it presented itself.

The aroma of baking bread and blooming flowers overwhelmed Anna's senses as she left the airport and the warm Andalusian sun greeted her. She was eager to start her experience in Granada, a city that skillfully combines its Moorish past with its Spanish background.

Anna immediately sensed the enchantment of the city as soon as she landed in Granada. She arrived at secret courtyards via meandering narrow streets surrounded by whitewashed buildings decorated with colourful flower pots. The courtyards were filled with the lovely echoes of Spanish guitar. While exploring these historic alleyways, Anna took in the bustling spirit of the city and found the distinctive hidden gems that define Granada.

The beautiful Alhambra Palace, a work of architecture embellished with delicate arabesques and lush gardens, was Anna's first trip. She savoured the complex intricacies and rich history that surrounded her as she walked through the palace's numerous halls, courtyards, and gardens. The Alhambra Palace was a reminder of Granada's colourful past, and Anna was happy to have had the chance to see it for herself.

But what captured Anna's heart in Granada were the hidden treasures. She happened to discover the Abuelo, an ancient Arab bath house hidden from the crowds of tourists. Here, Anna was able to lose herself in age-old traditions and forget about the outside world.

She also came to the Corral del Carbón, a stunningly maintained inn from the fourteenth century that previously hosted tired travellers on the Silk Road. The voyage of Anna was made more exciting and mysterious by these undiscovered gems.

Indulging in the regional cuisine is a must in any travel guide, and Granada is no exception. Anna was excited to sample the local cuisine and find the best tapas bars, where each drink was accompanied by a free small plate of delectables. Anna tasted the genuine essence of Andalusian food, from eating a steaming pan of paella to savouring the subtle flavours of Salmorejo.

But Granada beckons you to go outside and take in its breathtaking natural beauty as well as immerse yourself in its fascinating history and culinary delights.

Anna unwound and soaking up the Mediterranean sun on the sun-kissed beaches of the Costa Tropical after hiking through the magnificent Sierra Nevada Mountains, where the hiking trails led to breathtaking vistas. Every traveller's preferences were catered to by the wide variety of outdoor pursuits and day tours available in Granada.

The book "Travel Guide To Granada 2023, Discover the Hidden Gems of Granada: Your Ultimate Travel Guide," which Anna was flipping through, brought back memories of the beautiful city she had just left. The guide was more than just a list of tourist destinations and useful tips; it was an invitation to travel deeply into the heart of Granada. It was an opportunity to explore centuries of history, find undiscovered gems, enjoy delectable cuisine, and make lifelong memories.

Anna was aware that she would eventually visit Granada. She would once more meander through the historic streets, following in the footsteps of long-gone civilizations and losing herself in the captivating appeal of the city. Before then,

GETTING TO KNOW GRANADA

Granada, a city nestled in the heart of Andalusia, Spain, is a destination that captivates the hearts of travellers from around the world. In this chapter, we will dive into the soul of Granada, studying its rich history, vibrant culture, weather, and transit alternatives. You will have a strong foundation for your journey through this magical city by the end of this chapter.

- **The past of Granada:** Explore Granada's fascinating past, from its earliest Moorish origins to its influence on Spanish culture. Uncover the tales of conquerors and kings, exploring how Granada has evolved throughout the centuries.

- **Granada's culture:** Immerse yourself in the unique cultural tapestry of Granada. Learn about the fusion of Spanish and Moorish influences in the city's traditions, music, and art. Gain insights into the local way of life and the customs that define Granada's unique cultural identity.

- **Climate and Weather:** Learn about the weather and climate of Granada before you set out on your tour. Learn about the best times to visit, what to expect in different seasons, and how to pack accordingly. Whether you prefer the warmth of summer or the crisp air of winter, Granada has something to offer throughout the year.

- **Getting Around Granada: With** the help of our in-depth Granada transportation guide, you can move around the city like a local. Learn about the convenience of taxis and rental cars while exploring the options for public transportation, such as buses and trams. Discover the best routes and tips for getting around the city efficiently, ensuring you make the most of your time in Granada.

You will have a better understanding of Granada's history, culture, climate, and transportation system by the end of this chapter.

With this information at your disposal, you will be well-equipped to enter the city's core and begin exploring its wonders and undiscovered gems. So, pack your bags, open your mind to new experiences, and get ready to embark on an unforgettable journey through Granada.

HISTORY OF GRANADA

Granada's history is a tapestry woven with the threads of ancient civilizations, each leaving its mark on the city's landscape and culture. To properly understand the richness of Granada, we must dive into its enthralling past.

The earliest known settlers in the region were the Iberians, who created a vibrant culture in the area. However, it was during the Moorish era that Granada's history took a drastic turn. In the 8th century, the Moors, led by Tarik ibn Ziyad, conquered the region and established the Emirate of Granada.

Granada flourished into a hub of art, science, and commerce while it was ruled by the Moors. It became famed for its spectacular palaces, exquisite gardens, and advanced irrigation systems. The pinnacle of Moorish architecture in Granada is undoubtedly the Alhambra Palace, constructed during the 13th and 14th centuries. Visitors are still in awe of it because of its breathtaking beauty, intricate detailing, and harmonious fusion of Islamic and Christian influences.

With notable kings like Muhammad I, Yusuf I, and Muhammad V, the Nasrid Dynasty saw the peak of the Kingdom of Granada. However, the Christian Reconquista, a series of campaigns by Christian kingdoms to retake the Iberian Peninsula, progressively encroached into Granada's territories.

The final chapter of Muslim rule in Granada unfolded in 1492 when King Ferdinand II of Aragon and Queen Isabella I of Castile, known as the Catholic Monarchs, ended the Reconquista by seizing the city. This marked the end of Al-Andalus and the beginning of a new era for Granada.

The Catholic Monarchs launched a program of religious conversion and cultural assimilation to increase their political clout. They ordered the Royal Chapel to serve as their final resting place and built the imposing Cathedral of Granada on the site of the former Great Mosque.

As Spain rose to become a powerful European nation, Granada's history developed further. The city experienced a flourishing period under Charles V, Holy Roman Emperor, who commissioned the construction of the Charles V Palace adjacent to the Alhambra.

In the ensuing decades, Granada saw phases of prosperity and fall, impacted by wars, governmental shifts, and economic developments. However, its rich historical and cultural value remained steadfast, attracting researchers, artists, and writers who sought inspiration from its beauty and mystique.

Granada still stands as a reminder of the various civilizations that shaped its history. Each year, millions of tourists travel to the city's UNESCO World Heritage sites, such as the Alhambra, the Albayzin district, and the Generalife Gardens, to take in the city's magnificent architecture and fascinating history.

We can better appreciate Granada's cultural tapestry if we are aware of the city's historical development. It is a place where ancient legacies meld with contemporary life, offering a unique and unforgettable experience for those who seek to explore its hidden treasures.

Culture of Granada

Granada is a cultural melting pot that displays the many influences of its lengthy history. A vibrant fusion of Moorish, Christian, and Jewish traditions define its culture, each of which contributes to the city's own identity.

The flamenco tradition is one of Granada's most distinguishing cultural features. Flamenco, a passionate and evocative art style that blends music, dance, and poetry, is known to have originated in this city.

The flamenco scene in Granada is thriving, with many tablaos (flamenco venues) located all around the city. Visitors can see flamenco in its most authentic form, performed by talented artists who personify the art form's ferocious essence.

The food scene of Granada is another facet of its cultural legacy. Moorish, Spanish, and Mediterranean flavours are used in the city's cuisine to create a unique synthesis of varied influences.

Local delicacies include pianos, a sweet pastry baked with sugar, cinnamon, and cream, as well as tapas, tiny plates of cuisine served with drinks. Locals congregate in the lively tapas and bars that line the streets of Granada to enjoy wonderful cuisine, wine, and company.

Granada's culture also includes music and dance. The city holds several festivals throughout the year that feature a variety of musical styles, from classical and jazz to traditional flamenco. One of the most prominent cultural events in Europe, the International Festival of Music and Dance annually takes place in the Alhambra Palace and draws world-famous performers.

The museums and galleries of Granada, which present a noteworthy collection of works by national and international artists, also represent the city's rich creative history. The Museum of Fine Arts, located in a palace from the 16th century, has a sizable collection of artwork from the Renaissance to the current age.

The Museum of Romanticism, which showcases decorative arts and furniture from the 19th century, is located in the lovely mansion Carmen de los Martires, which is surrounded by lush gardens.

Throughout its history, religion and spirituality have been integral parts of Granada's culture. The numerous churches, monasteries, and convents throughout the city, which are influenced by Catholicism, are a testament to its rich religious history. Granada's patron saint, Saint Caecilius, is honoured at the Sacromonte Abbey, a renowned pilgrimage site built on a hill overlooking the city.

Granada is mostly a Catholic city, but it also has a sizable Muslim and Jewish population. With its winding lanes and whitewashed homes, the Albaicin area originally served as the centre of Granada's Muslim population.

It is now a thriving, multiethnic area where tourists may study Moorish architecture, eat Middle Eastern food, and visit mosques and other Islamic attractions. With its winding alleyways, charming squares, and antique synagogues, the Jewish Quarter in the Realejo district of Granada is another example of the city's eclectic legacy.

In general, the culture of Granada is a complex tapestry of history, art, music, and spirituality that reflects the various influences of its past. Its residents take pride in their city's distinctive identity and celebrate and maintain its traditions and customs. Granada's elegance, culture, and hospitality are likely to wow visitors.

Weather and Climate

The climate and weather in Granada give this magical city an added degree of attraction. Granada, located in southern Spain's Andalusia area, has a Mediterranean climate with warm summers, mild winters, and a lot of sunshine all year round.

- Long, sunny days and pleasant temperatures characterise Granada's summer (June to August). Between 30°C (86°F) and 35°C (95°F), the average high temperature makes it the ideal time to see the city's outdoor attractions and take part in the bustling street life.

  It's important to remember that the summer also sees an increase in visitor activity, so plan on seeing more people at popular locations.

- Granada experiences moderate temperatures and gentler weather in the spring (March to May) and fall (September to November). With milder evenings, average high temperatures vary from 20°C (68°F) to 25°C (77°F).

The weather is pleasant during these seasons, making it possible to wander through the city's gardens, explore its historic buildings, and engage in outdoor activities.

- Although Granada's winter (December to February) is typically moderate, it can occasionally be colder than the rest of the year. 10°C (50°F) to 15°C (59°F) is the typical range for daily temperatures, with cooler evenings and sporadic showers. Winter in Granada offers a calmer ambiance, fewer queues at attractions, and the chance to partake in the city's joyous holiday customs, even though it might not be as warm as other seasons.

- The proximity of the Sierra Nevada Mountains to Granada, which affects local weather patterns, is one distinctive feature of the region's climate. The mountains not only make a beautiful backdrop, but they also present fantastic chances for those who love winter sports.

  Depending on snow conditions, the nearby Sierra Nevada Ski Resort offers skiing and snowboarding opportunities from late November to early May.

- It is advised to carry layers for your trip to Granada because the weather might change throughout the day, especially in the transitional seasons. In this season, you should always wear comfortable walking shoes, a hat, sunglasses, and sunscreen because the sun can be very powerful.

Overall, Granada's environment and weather make for a comfortable setting for taking in the city's historical attractions, delectable cuisine, and vibrant culture. Granada greets you with open arms and is prepared to amaze you with its appeal in any season, whether you like the warmth of summer, the mildness of spring and autumn, or the tranquillity of winter.

Getting Around Granada

It may be exciting just to go around a new city, and Granada is no exception. Thankfully, Granada has a variety of transportation choices to make it simple for you to easily tour the city and its surroundings. To help you make the most of your time in Granada, we will walk you through the numerous transportation options in this chapter.

- **Using Public Transit:** Buses and trams are part of the effective public transit system of Granada. The bus network is a practical way to get around since it covers the entire city and its surroundings.

  Tickets can be bought from the bus driver or at specified ticket machines, and buses run from early in the morning until late at night. Keep an eye out for the citywide highly identifiable blue and white buses.

- The Metro de Granada, often known as the Granada Tram, is a cutting-edge light rail network that links several parts of the city. It offers a convenient and efficient means of transportation, especially over longer distances. Tickets can be purchased at tram stations or via ticket vending machines, and the tram runs from early in the morning until midnight.

- **Taxis:** In Granada, taxis are widely available and provide a practical and effective form of transportation, particularly for shorter distances or when travelling with large amounts of luggage. Taxis can be located at designated taxi ranks or hailed from the street anywhere in the city. Before beginning your trip, make sure the taxi has a functional taximeter. You could also ask for an estimate of the fee to avoid any unpleasant surprises.

- **Car rentals:** Renting a car in Granada is an option worth considering if you value freedom and owning a car. The city and the airport both have several car rental companies that provide a selection of vehicles to meet your needs.

  With a car, you can travel outside of the city to explore the surroundings. It's necessary to become familiar with the city's traffic laws and regulations, as well as the restrictions and requirements for parking.

- **Cycling and Walking:** The greatest way to see Granada is on foot, especially in its old-town areas. You may take in the splendour of the city, find hidden jewels, and take in the vibrant atmosphere by walking. The Alhambra and Albayzin are just two of the popular sights that are conveniently reachable on foot.

- In Granada, cycling is also a common form of transportation, and the city provides visitors with bike rental options. Cycling is a safe and pleasurable way to explore the city and its surroundings thanks to dedicated bike lanes and trails. Granada is a hilly city, so be prepared for some uphill cycling.

- **A day trip:** The central location of Granada within Andalusia makes it a great starting point for day visits to adjacent locations. There are many possibilities, ranging from the breathtaking Alpujarra mountain towns to the charming city of Cordoba or the magnificent Costa Tropical coastline. Depending on your choices and comfort level, think about using public transit to get to these places or joining a guided tour.

Granada has a variety of transit choices, making travelling easy and convenient. Whether you decide to travel around the city on foot, by bus, tram, taxi, rental car, or any other means of transportation, each mode of mobility offers a distinctive perspective and heightens the experience of finding Granada's hidden gems. So get a map, hop on your preferred mode of transportation, and start exploring.

TOP SIGHTS AND ATTRACTIONS

Granada, a city brimming with history, culture, and stunning beauty, offers a wide variety of sights to view and activities to partake in. This fascinating city offers a wealth of sights to see and things to do, from Alhambra's famous architecture to the lovely lanes of the Albayzin.

To assist you in creating your schedule, we will highlight some of the main landmarks and attractions of Granada in this chapter.

- **Alhambra:** The Alhambra, one of Spain's most well-known attractions, is a must-see if visiting Granada. Beautiful gardens, amazing architecture, and elaborate sculptures can be found throughout this magnificent palace and castle complex, which was built in the 13th century. While admiring the wide views of the city below, guests are welcome to explore the palace, gardens, and castle walls. As Alhambra is a popular tourist destination, tickets must be ordered in advance because they frequently sell out.

- **Albayzin:** The Albayzin, a Middle Ages ancient neighbourhood, is known by its whitewashed houses, winding alleyways, and breath-taking Alhambra views.

  Visitors can explore the neighbourhood on foot while taking in the beautiful architecture and stopping at one of the many cafes and restaurants along the way. The Mirador de San Nicolas, which overlooks the Alhambra, is a popular spot to watch the sun set.

- **Sacromonte:** Flamenco performances and cave dwellings are well-known features of the Sacromonte region. Visitors can explore the neighbourhood on foot while taking in the unusual architecture and stopping by one of the many flamenco venues to catch a performance.

  The Cuevas del Sacromonte Museum, which showcases regional history and culture, is a worthwhile trip.

- **The Granada Cathedral:** In the centre of the city stands the magnificent Renaissance building known as the Granada Cathedral, also known as the Cathedral of the Incarnation. The Royal Chapel, which contains the tombs of Queen Isabella and King Ferdinand, is one of the cathedral's notable pieces of architectural and artistic beauty.

- **Generalife:** The Generalife, a set of gardens next to the Alhambra, is home to exquisite fountains, terraces, and flowers. The tranquil atmosphere and breathtaking views of the Alhambra can be experienced by guests while strolling through the gardens.

- **Analysis Park:** The Science Park of Granada is a museum and science centre that welcomes visitors of all ages. The centre's features include a planetarium, a butterfly house, and interactive exhibits.

- **The Royal Chapel in Granada:** In close proximity to the Granada Cathedral lies the Gothic-style church known as the Royal Chapel of Granada. Along with other members of the royal family, the tombs of Queen Isabella and King Ferdinand are located in the chapel.

- **Martires, Carmen:** A lovely park called Carmen de los Martires was constructed on a hilltop with city views. The park, which has a miniature palace, statues, and fountains, provides breathtaking views of the Alhambra and the surroundings.

- **Fine Arts Gallery:** Spanish art from the 15th to the 20th century is on display in the Museum of Fine Arts of Granada, a must-see destination for art enthusiasts. The museum is set in a beautiful Renaissance building and offers visitors a peek into Spain's renowned artistic heritage.

- **Carrera del Darro:** Enjoy a leisurely stroll along this charming roadway that traces the path of the Darro River. Admire the beautiful homes, historic bridges, and breathtaking vistas of the Albaicin area and the Alhambra.

These must-see places in Granada provide a wide range of experiences, from taking in the city's rich culture to discovering its stunning natural surroundings. Every one of them adds to the distinctive attraction and charm of this enchanting Spanish city.

Alhambra Palace and Generalife Gardens

The Alhambra Palace and Generalife Gardens are two of Granada's most recognizable and magnificent sites. A representation of the city's historic heritage and stunning architecture, this UNESCO World Heritage site.

The spectacular palace complex known as the Alhambra Palace, often referred to as the Red Fortress, was built in the fourteenth century. The Nasrid dynasty, the final Moorish monarchy in Spain, lived there.

The palace showcases the exquisite Islamic architecture with decorative stucco carvings, elaborate tilework, and geometric designs. You will be taken back in time to the era of Moorish splendour as you move through its halls, courtyards, and gardens.

The focal point of the Alhambra Palace is a collection of buildings known as the Nasrid Palaces. A lovely fountain with 12 marble lions that decorate it may be found in the centre courtyard of the Palace of the Lions, which is very alluring.

The Palace of the Mexuar, Palace of Comares, and Palace of the Partal are equally magnificent structures that each include unique architectural features and stunning panoramas of the surroundings.

The Alhambra Palace is next to the Generalife Gardens, a paradise of rich foliage, alluring flowers, and tranquil water features. The Nasrid kings used the gardens as a getaway spot for recreation, offering them a tranquil and beautiful haven. Beautiful terraces, shady pathways, and immaculately kept lawns can all be found as you stroll around the Generalife Gardens. Don't skip the Patio de la Acequia, a plaza with beautiful fountains and water features that fosters a calm and relaxing atmosphere.

Aside from the Alhambra Palace, the Generalife Gardens also provide breathtaking views of Granada. From certain viewing points, you can see the splendour of the palace with the Sierra Nevada Mountains in the distance, creating a truly breathtaking scene.

A must-do while in Granada is to visit the Generalife Gardens and Alhambra Palace, but planning your trip ahead of time is essential. Tickets to the Alhambra frequently sell out quickly due to its popularity, especially during peak travel times. To guarantee your visit, you must buy your tickets online well in advance.

You will be mesmerised by the Alhambra Palace's beauty, history, and artistic merit. You'll develop a greater understanding of the architectural skill and cultural value of this amazing monument as you stroll around its lovely rooms and gardens.

Cathedral of Granada and Royal Chapel

The Granada Cathedral and the nearby Royal Chapel are important landmarks in the city. These architectural wonders store significant historical relics and provide a window into the city's religious history.

A remarkable example of Spanish Renaissance architecture is the Cathedral of Granada, often known as the Cathedral of the Incarnation. The cathedral's building process started in 1523 and lasted for more than 180 years. With beautiful stone carvings and complex facades, the cathedral's exterior is a remarkable fusion of Gothic and Renaissance styles.

You'll be welcomed by a majestic interior of the cathedral when you enter it, complete with soaring columns, lovely chapels, and complex stained glass windows. With its soaring height and elaborate workmanship, the middle nave is especially breathtaking. Numerous works of art, including historical paintings, sculptures, and religious items, may be found inside the Cathedral of Granada.

The Royal Chapel of Granada, a mausoleum that is connected to the cathedral, serves as the final resting place for some of Spain's most significant historical leaders.

Queen Isabella I of Castile and King Ferdinand II of Aragon, who were instrumental in the unification of Spain and the conclusion of the Reconquista, were buried in the chapel, which was constructed between 1505 and 1521. The centrepiece of the chapel are its elaborate alabaster graves.

Joanna of Castile and her husband, Philip the Handsome, are buried in the Royal Chapel between the tombs of

Queen Isabella and King Ferdinand. Beautiful paintings, sculptures, and beautifully carved altarpieces are among the sacred artefacts and works of fine art that embellish the chapel's interior.

Exploring the city's religious and historical past can be done by visiting the Royal Chapel and the Cathedral of Granada. The elaborate structures, magnificent artwork, and royal tombs provide a fascinating look into the lives of the historical personalities who had a significant impact on Granada.

The cathedral and the chapel may have different schedules, so be sure to check them both while making travel arrangements. To gain a deeper understanding of the significance and history of these outstanding structures, guided tours are offered.

As you awe at the architectural magnificence of the Cathedral of

Granada and pay respect to the significant personalities interred in the Royal Chapel, immerse yourself in the rich cultural and historical fabric of Granada. These outstanding landmarks serve as a reminder of the city's history and provide tourists with an unforgettable experience.

Albayzin Neighborhood and Mirador de San Nicolas

The Albayzin district, a charming and historically significant enclave that captures the spirit of the city's Moorish heritage, is located in the centre of Granada.

You'll feel as though you've been transported back in time as you meander through its meandering, tiny lanes, passing whitewashed homes, cobblestone pathways, and breathtaking views at every turn.

The Albayzin was once the home of the Muslim people of Granada during the Middle Ages. The area has kept a lot of its original beauty and character, and its confusing layout shows the Moorish influence. You'll come across stunning architectural gems, secret plazas, and charming stores selling local handicrafts and mementos while strolling around the Albayzin.

The Mirador de San Nicolas, a scenic vantage point with expansive views of the Alhambra Palace and the city of Granada, is one of the highlights of the Albayzin. The Mirador de San Nicolas, which is situated at the top of the Albayzin, is a popular place for locals and tourists to congregate and take in the spectacular scenery.

You'll be welcomed by a bustling square with cafes, street performers, and vendors selling their wares as you get closer to the Mirador de San Nicolas. Choose a position on one of the stone steps or benches, and be ready to be mesmerised by the scene in front of you. The grand Alhambra Palace is visible in the distance, shining brightly in both the daytime and nighttime illuminations. The stunning backdrop of the Sierra

Nevada Mountains completes the lovely image.

The Alhambra and the city below are illuminated by a mystical glow at sunset, which is one of the most beautiful times to visit the Mirador de San Nicolas. As musicians play upbeat music and painters depict the beauty of the surroundings on their canvases, the mood becomes even more upbeat.

In addition to its breathtaking views, the Mirador de San Nicolas provides a window into Granada's thriving cultural scene. Flamenco performances are frequently held here, offering an enthralling display of traditional music and dance against the Alhambra's backdrop. The actors' vigour and emotion, along with the stunning scenery, make for an amazing experience.

The Mirador de San Nicolas and the Albayzin area are like stepping into a picture-perfect scene. A sense of timeless beauty and serenity is created by the winding alleys, whitewashed homes, and breathtaking views.

The Albayzin and the Mirador de San Nicolas will create a lasting impression on your trip to Granada, whether you're admiring the Alhambra, enjoying a cup of coffee at a neighbourhood café, or immersing yourself in the dynamic cultural environment.

Sacromonte Caves

The Sacromonte district, located in the hills above Granada, is a distinctive and fascinating place known for its cave dwellings and rich flamenco legacy. The Sacromonte Caves are like entering a secret world with echoes of the city's past.

The Sacromonte area has a historical history that dates back to the 16th century, when the Romani people, sometimes known as gipsies, settled there. These industrious people built their dwellings into the mountainside over time, forming a remarkable cave settlement that still exists today. Some of these "cuevas," as they are known locally, have been passed down through the centuries.

The Sacromonte Caves provide a window into the distinctive way of life and cultural legacy of the Romani people. You'll run into a maze of tiny courtyards, cave openings, and winding alleyways as you explore the area. The sharp contrast between the untamed nature and the whitewashed cave façade makes for a gorgeous and intriguing scene.

Flamenco is another practice that has a long history in the Sacromonte district. The intimate atmosphere and excellent acoustics of the caves make them the ideal location for this passionate and emotional art form.

Many of the caves have been converted into flamenco theatres, giving guests the chance to see real performances in a cosy and immersive environment. An extraordinary sensation is created by the rhythmic clapping, sincere singing, and eerie guitar notes that reverberate throughout the caves.

A trip to the Cuevas del Sacromonte Museum is essential for people who want to learn more about the history and culture of the area. The museum, which is housed inside a renovated cave residence, offers insights into the daily lives of the cave occupants and features relics, images, and multimedia presentations that emphasise the neighbourhood's legacy.

Discovering hidden treasures while meandering through the winding streets of the Sacromonte Caves is part of the experience in and of itself. People looking to fully immerse themselves in Granada's history and traditions find the district to be a fascinating destination because of its authenticity and rich cultural tapestry.

You'll sense a link to the past and an admiration for the resourcefulness and vivacious spirit of the Sacromonte neighbourhood's residents as soon as you enter. The Sacromonte Caves offer a distinctive and unforgettable experience in Granada, whether you're intrigued by the cave architecture, enthralled by the soul-stirring flamenco performances, or simply enthralled by the beauty of the area.

Carmen de los Mártires

Carmen de los Martires is a hidden gem that encourages tourists to immerse themselves in a serene refuge of natural beauty and historical charm. It is perched on a magnificent hillside overlooking the city of Granada. This beautiful garden serves as a reminder of the city's extensive historical and cultural legacy.

Originally, Carmen de los Martires was a wealthy 19th-century aristocratic family's private estate. It is now a public park that enthrals visitors with its lush foliage, heavenly flowers, and breathtaking views. You'll feel calm and as though you've stepped back in time as soon as you enter the garden.

Elegant fountains, winding paths, colourful flower beds, and towering trees that offer welcome shade on hot days are just a few of the garden's harmoniously combined features. Every nook and cranny of Carmen de los Martires offers a new thrill, from wide areas great for picnics and strolls to quiet corners ideal for quiet reflection.

The tiny palace that adorns the garden's grounds is one of its features. The Palace of Dona Ana, a neo-gothic building, gives the atmosphere a sense of opulence and elegance. It serves as a pleasant garden focal point because of its exquisite architectural design and elaborate detailing.

You'll come across a gorgeous pond with swans and water lilies as you continue your exploration. Visitors are encouraged to take a seat, unwind, and take in the calm ambiance while listening to the relaxing sounds of flowing water at this serene location.

Additionally, Carmen de los Martires provides enthralling views of the surroundings. You'll be rewarded with expansive views of the city of Granada, the Alhambra Palace, and the magnificent Sierra Nevada Mountains in the distance from specific vantage points within the garden. These spectacular views add a dash of unmatched beauty to the already charming scene.

Carmen de los Martires, the name of the garden, has a distinguished past. It alludes to the neighbouring Alhambra, the alleged site of the martyrdom of Christians under Muslim control. This highlights the garden's function as a tranquil sanctuary in the middle of a violent history and adds a fascinating element of historical relevance to it.

Granada's busy downtown streets provide a lovely diversion when you visit Carmen de los Martires. It provides a peaceful haven where people may commune with nature, take in the beauty of their surroundings, and think back on the fascinating history that has built this great city.

Carmen de los Martires is a secret paradise that will make a lasting impression on your trip to Granada, whether you're looking for a quiet getaway, a romantic setting, or simply a place to unwind and appreciate the beauty of nature.

HIDDEN GEMS

With its fascinating past and thriving present, Granada is a city full of undiscovered treasures just waiting to be found. There are interesting and lesser-known locations outside of the well-known attractions that provide a look into the true character of the city. Here are a few Granada attractions worth checking out:

- One of the oldest still-standing structures in Granada is the Corral del Carbón, a Moorish inn from the 14th century that is tucked away in the heart of the city.

  With its magnificent courtyard, graceful arches, and detailed features, the city's past is revealed. It now functions as a cultural hub and frequently holds performances and art exhibitions.

- El Bauelo is a well-preserved 11th-century Arab bathhouse that will transport you back to antiquity. El Bauelo, with its exquisitely maintained architecture, including its marble columns and domed ceilings, provides a unique look into historical bathing customs.

- **Carmen de los Mártires:** This secret garden provides a tranquil retreat from the busy city and is close to the Alhambra. The garden is filled with lush vegetation, tranquil ponds, and breathtaking views of Granada. It's the perfect place for a quiet picnic or a stroll away from the bustle.

- Federico Garcia Lorca spent his summers in this picturesque house, Huerta de San Vicente. His artwork was inspired by the serene gardens that surrounded the estate. The poet's home is now accessible to the public, giving people a chance to peek inside and learn more about his life and artistic legacy.

- **Paseo de los Tristes:** Situated at the foot of the Alhambra, this charming promenade provides breathtaking views of both the fortress and the surroundings. It's the ideal area to take a stroll, enjoy a delectable meal, or just take in the beauty of the surroundings because it is lined with bright cafes and tiny stores.

- The network of caves known as Sacromonte Abbey perched atop the Sacromonte hill, has been converted into a place of worship. The monastery provides insight into the local culture and history, and its expansive terrace affords stunning views of Granada and the Alhambra.

- **Plaza Larga:** This bustling square is the centre of local activities and is situated in the Albayzin area. It provides an opportunity to experience daily life in Granada thanks to its vibrant market booths, charming cafes, and genuine atmosphere.

For those looking to explore Granada's off-the-beaten-path attractions and discover its hidden gems, these hidden gems provide a distinctive and uncommon experience.

These less well-known locations provide a deeper insight into Granada's culture, history, and natural beauty. They range from historical sites to peaceful gardens and charming neighbourhoods. Explore this mesmerising city's streets and corners away from the usual tourist routes to uncover its enchanted secrets.

The Bañuelo

The Bauelo is a hidden jewel that takes visitors back to the time of Moorish rule and is tucked away among the historic alleyways of Granada. The Nasrid dynasty, which formerly predominated in the city, was incredibly inventive and sophisticated, as evidenced by this architectural wonder, also known as the Arab Baths.

One of the oldest and best preserved Arab bath complexes in Spain, the Bauelo is situated in the centre of Granada's Albaicin area and dates back to the 11th century. You will be greeted by a fascinating world of beauty and calm as soon as you enter via its modest entryway.

The Bauelo is made up of several rooms, each of which serves a certain function in the traditional bathing process. The architecture contains typical Islamic components like marble columns, horseshoe-shaped arches, and elaborate stucco work. The Moors were master builders, as seen by their fine workmanship and attention to detail.

You'll come across many bathing chambers as you explore the Abuelo, each with its special characteristics. The tepidarium, a warm area, is offered as a place to unwind and get the body ready for the cleansing routine.

Visitors could make use of the therapeutic benefits of steam and hot water in the steam bath located in the hot room, or caldarium. After the stifling heat of the caldarium, the cool room, or frigidarium, gave a soothing plunge into cold water.

As you go through the Abuelo, you'll be enthralled by the way that light and shadow play off each other on the old walls, resulting in a tranquil and mystical ambiance. Your journey will have a calming soundtrack added by the fountains' trickling water, which will transport you to a bygone period.

The value of the Bauelo goes beyond its aesthetic appeal. It provides a look into the customs and way of life of those who formerly lived in this thriving city. The baths were a gathering area for people to interact, unwind, and have thought-provoking conversations in addition to being a location for physical purification.

The Bauelo is a historical landmark where entering it is like entering a time capsule filled with echoes of the past. It enables you to appreciate the Moors' astounding accomplishments in the arts, sciences, and culture.

You might find yourself thinking about how Granada's identity was fashioned by the peaceful coexistence of several cultures as you leave Abuelo. This undiscovered treasure welcomes you to learn more about the city's fascinating past and serves as a reminder of its unique multicultural heritage.

Therefore, when visiting Granada, be sure to put the Bauelo on your agenda. You can connect with the past and gain an appreciation for the architectural and cultural legacy of this wonderful city through the unique and rewarding experience it offers.

The Corral del Carbón

Tucked away amid the bustling streets of Granada sits a hidden jewel of Moorish architecture and historical significance—the Corral del Carbón. This charming courtyard provides a window into the city's vivacious past and is a testament to its enduring cultural legacy thanks to its rich history and alluring charm.

The Corral del Carbón, which dates back to the 14th century, was formerly a thriving commercial centre and a rest stop for weary travellers. This Moorish inn, or caravanserai, provided shelter for traders and their products as they went along the historic Silk Road. Today, it stands as the oldest surviving caravanserai in Spain, a rare gem that has withstood the test of time.

As you step into the Corral del Carbón, you are immediately transported to a different era. The focus of this architectural marvel is the spectacular courtyard, embellished with exquisite arches, elaborate plasterwork, and a peaceful central fountain. The Nasrid dynasty made an indelible impression on the architectural landscape of Granada, and the symmetrical design and fine details demonstrate their mastery.

Beyond its architectural allure, the Corral del Carbón holds a vibrant history. It previously served as a thriving hub for trade and business, drawing traders from all over the globe to exchange commodities and concepts. The inn provided a key link between East and West, serving as a vital halt for caravans as they travelled the region.

The Corral del Carbón has been transformed into a cultural hub today, allowing guests to become fully immersed in the artistic and musical traditions of the city. The courtyard frequently hosts musical events, theatrical productions, and art exhibits, giving fresh life to this historic location and encouraging creativity.

Visiting the Corral del Carbón is a rare opportunity to observe the legacy of Granada's varied past. It invites you to explore the nooks and crannies of the courtyard, visualising the vivid scenes of hustling merchants and cultural exchange that once took place within its walls. Take a minute to sit beneath the shadow of the arches, letting your imagination transport you to a bygone era.

As you depart the Corral del Carbón, you may find yourself musing on the beauty and tenacity of Granada's cultural history. This hidden jewel serves as a reminder of the city's rich past, its connections to other civilizations, and its ability to reinvent itself while keeping its traditions.

So, make sure to add the Corral del Carbón to your schedule when exploring Granada. Discover the appeal of this architectural marvel, embrace the echoes of the past, and immerse yourself in the vibrant cultural tapestry that defines this extraordinary city.

The Casa-Museo Max Moreau

Nestled within the picturesque alleyways of Granada, the Casa-Museo Max Moreau stands as a hidden gem, enticing art fans and curious visitors alike.

This engaging museum, dedicated to the great Belgian artist Max Moreau, offers a unique and personal view into his life, artistic career, and the enchanting universe he created.

As soon as you enter the Casa-Museo Max Moreau, an atmosphere of inspiration and imagination surrounds you. The experience is made more intimate by the fact that the museum is housed inside a historic structure that originally functioned as Moreau's dwelling. The room has been meticulously organised to exhibit Moreau's varied body of work, spanning from paintings and sculptures to sketches and ceramics.

Max Moreau is well-known for his particular style, which combines aspects of magical realism, symbolism, and surrealism. His dreamlike and whimsical works of art have caught the attention of audiences. Visitors are drawn into a world where fiction and reality coexist thanks to his meticulous attention to detail, brilliant colour scheme, and fantastical motifs.

You'll come across a rich tapestry of Moreau's artistic expressions as you explore the Casa-Museo. Paintings filled with ethereal landscapes, mysterious people, and significant elements inspire you to dig further into his artistic vision. The sculptures display Moreau's talent for giving inanimate objects life through their beautiful forms and flawless craftsmanship.

Beyond the actual artworks, the Casa-Museo Max Moreau provides a chance to explore the artist's home and learn about his creative process. Moreau's studio, complete with his brushes, paints, and easels, is preserved in the museum. Visitors can establish a stronger connection with the artist and gain insight into his inspiration thanks to this look into his workspace.

You can find yourself enthralled by the narratives that each piece of art tells as you move through the museum. From whimsical scenes that transport you to enchanted regions to thought-provoking symbolism that invites contemplation, Moreau's creations arouse emotions and generate a sense of wonder.

The Casa-Museo Max Moreau is more than just a collection of priceless works of art; it is a celebration of the creative spirit and the strength of the imagination. It enables guests to delve into the depths of their imagination and be carried away to a world where the lines between fantasy and reality are hazy.

Therefore, when visiting Granada, be sure to add a stop at the Casa-Museo Max Moreau in your plans. Discover the beauty in this visionary artist's works, become lost in his intriguing world, and let your imagination fly.

The El Huerto Juan Ranas

The El Huerto de Juan Ranas is a secret haven of elegance and peace located high in the hills of Granada's Albaicin district, overlooking the magnificent Alhambra. Offering a haven from the busy streets below, this charming terrace and restaurant welcome guests to appreciate fine cuisine while taking in the spectacular views of Granada's famous attractions.

You'll discover this hidden treasure buried behind a modest facade as you traverse the twisting streets of the Albaicin. It feels like entering a secret paradise when you step onto the patio of El Huerto de Juan Ranas since there are aromatic flowers, luscious vegetation, and trickling fountains that create a tranquil and secluded atmosphere.

The terrace itself provides an unrivalled vantage point to take in the splendour of the Alhambra. With its rich architectural intricacies and breathtaking beauty on full show, the mighty fortress appears to be just a hand's reach away. The Alhambra is bathed in a golden glow as the sun sets and reflects its warm colours across the landscape, creating a stunning picture.

The food at El Huerto de Juan Ranas is also a gourmet marvel, so it's not just about the vistas. With a focus on fresh, regional ingredients, the restaurant's menu features the best of Andalusian cuisine. Every bite is a monument to the region's gastronomic legacy, from traditional tapas brimming with flavour to inventive meals that combine classic recipes with a modern flair.

Enjoy a meal of rich and flavorful salmorejo, some luscious Iberian ham, or some delectable seafood that showcases the riches of the adjacent Mediterranean Sea. Let your dinner transport you to the heart of Andalusia by sipping on a great Spanish wine or a crisp local craft beer while you eat.

El Huerto de Juan Ranas is unique due to its atmosphere as well as its cuisine and scenery. The terrace has cosy sofas, soft lighting, and rustic wooden furnishings to create a welcoming and laid-back ambiance. The atmosphere is ideal for making enduring memories, whether you're having a romantic dinner, catching up with friends, or just relaxing with a cocktail as the sun goes down.

You'll realise why this undiscovered gem has won the hearts of both locals and tourists as you linger on the patio of El Huerto de Juan Ranas, soaking in the stunning vistas and savouring the mouth watering flavours. It provides an opportunity to escape the city's noise and bustle and revel in a little moment of peace and beauty in Granada.

So when seeing Granada, be sure to add El Huerto de Juan Ranas to your schedule. Discover the mystique of this secret paradise, allow the vistas to take your breath away, and let the flavours of Andalusia tempt your palate.

.

The Parque de las Ciencias

The Parque de las Ciencias is a sizable and captivating science park that welcomes visitors of all ages and is situated in the centre of Granada. For those looking for a distinctive and enlightening experience, this hidden gem is a must-visit location since it mixes education, entertainment, and innovation.

You will be welcomed by a vivid and immersive setting that piques curiosity and stokes the imagination as soon as you enter the Parque de las Ciencias. The park offers a wide variety of interesting displays, hands-on activities, and interactive exhibits that explore a range of scientific fields, from physics and biology to astronomy and technology.

A voyage through the universe awaits you at the planetarium, where you can discover the mysteries of space and awe at the wonders of the universe. At the interactive biology exhibits, you may learn about anatomy, genetics, and the complexities of life itself while also discovering the wonders of the human body. Participate in experiments and shows that highlight the laws of physics, chemistry, and electricity to inspire awe and wonder.

Through the inclusion of outdoor areas that perfectly merge science and nature, the Parque de las Ciencias goes beyond the bounds of standard museum visits. Discover the Botanical Garden, a tranquil haven that stresses the value of environmental conservation while showcasing a wide variety of plant species.

Visit outdoor exhibitions, such as the Water Pavilion or the Astronomical Observation Terrace, to learn about sustainable methods and the significance of protecting our natural resources.

The famous butterfly house, where you may lose yourself in a tropical haven of fluttering wings and brilliant colours, is one of the park's highlights. Enter this magical ecosystem to see these delicate creatures going about their daily lives up close. It's a wonderfully enthralling experience that makes you aware of nature's marvels.

A wide range of temporary exhibitions, educational seminars, and cultural activities are also held at the Parque de las Ciencias, which further improves the tourist experience. In the park's dynamic and ever-changing environment, there is always something new and intriguing to explore, from art installations and photography exhibitions to scientific conferences and educational events.

The Parque de las Ciencias offers plenty of leisure areas for guests to unwind, have picnics, or just take in tranquil settings in addition to its educational programs. The park's well-maintained gardens, lovely ponds, and shady walks provide a tranquil haven from the bustle of the city.

More than just a science museum, the Parque de las Ciencias offers you the ability to pique your interest, increase your knowledge, and participate in experiential learning. It is a location where science is brought to life, where innovation and nature coexist, and where the wonders of the globe are made accessible to everyone.

So when travelling to Granada, be sure to include the Parque de las Ciencias in your schedule. Explore this fascinating hidden gem, lose yourself in the wonders of science and nature, and experience the thrill of discovery.

FOOD AND DRINK

Food enthusiasts will find paradise in Granada, which offers a great variety of flavours that honour the area's long culinary tradition. The city's culinary offerings, which range from classic Spanish meals to distinctive Andalusian delicacies, are sure to excite your palate and leave you wanting more.

Consuming tapas is one of the must-do gastronomic experiences in Granada. In Granada, unlike many other areas, tapas are frequently provided without charge when you order a drink at a bar or restaurant.

By participating in this custom, you can try a variety of small plates that are all brimming with flavour. Tapas in Granada are a true culinary journey, with everything from traditional choices like patatas bravas (fried potatoes with a spicy sauce) and jamón ibérico (cured ham) to regional specialties like pescadito frito (fried fish) and migas (a hearty meal made with breadcrumbs and various spices).

There are several restaurants in Granada that offer the best of both regional and Spanish cuisine for those looking for a more formal dining experience. Traditional foods like paella, gazpacho, and rabo de toro, which are frequently created using ingredients found locally and cooked with love and passion, are available for you to enjoy.

Fresh seafood from the adjacent Mediterranean Sea will thrill seafood fans, while meat lovers can savour sumptuous cuts of grilled or roasted meats, such chuletón (ribeye steak) or cordero al horno (oven-roasted lamb).

Make sure to sample the regional wines and spirits to go with your meal. Wines from the adjacent La Alpujarra region, which is recognized for producing flavorful wines, are especially popular in Granada. The surrounding vineyards offer a variety of wines that go well with the cuisine of the area, from clean whites to strong reds. If you'd like something stronger, try a glass of the powerful anise-flavoured local aguardiente, which is sometimes consumed as a digestif.

No trip to Granada's restaurants would be complete without indulging in some of the city's sweet offerings. One of the most recognizable pastries from Granada is the pionono. A little, cylindrical sponge cake filled with cream and coated with powdered sugar makes up this delectable treat. It is a wonderful joy for your taste buds thanks to its smooth texture and sweet flavours.

Try the well-known tarta de la almohada, a pillow-shaped tart baked with almonds, honey, and a touch of cinnamon, for a cool treat on a hot day. Its nutty and mild flavours are the ideal way to cap off a full meal.

Granada offers a culinary experience that will make a lasting impression, whether you're dining in the city centre, strolling through the narrow lanes of the Albaicin, or looking for undiscovered local jewels. So embrace the pleasures of this lively city, enjoy the regional specialties, and let Granada's culinary treasures entice your taste buds.

Typical dishes and drinks of Granada

With a rich culinary past, Granada provides a great selection of regional foods and beverages that are sure to please even the most discriminating palate. Here are some of the city's culinary delicacies that you simply must try:

- The distinctive and tasty Tortilla de Sacromonte is a regional specialty. It incorporates offal, such as brain, liver, and kidneys, with the typical Spanish tortilla (an omelette made with eggs and potatoes). Although it may sound daring, the fusion of flavours and textures results in a very unforgettable experience.

- **Plato Alpujarreo:** This robust cuisine, which originates from the nearby Alpujarra region, highlights the tastes of the highlands. It often consists of a delectable combination of fried eggs, potatoes, ham, and sliced sausage (such as Spanish chorizo or morcilla). It is a full and fulfilling dish that showcases the region's rustic and age-old culinary customs.

- **Habas with Jamón:** This straightforward yet tasty dish is made with soft fava beans and cured ham. A delectable flavour combination is produced by combining savoury ham with earthy beans. It is a well-liked option for a tapa or side dish.

- **Pionono:** A delectable treat you must not miss, the piano is a true icon of Granada's pastry sector. It is made up of a little, cylindrical sponge cake that is filled with cream and sprinkled with sugar. It is popular among both locals and visitors due to its delicate texture and decadent flavours.

- While gazpacho is a common meal in all of Andalusia, the version from Granada is particularly deserving of note. Ripe tomatoes, cucumbers, peppers, garlic, olive oil, and vinegar are used to make this chilled tomato soup. It is tasty, energising, and ideal for cooling off on a warm summer day.

- Granada provides a variety of drinks to go along with your meal or to enjoy on their own:

- **Tinto de Verano:** This cool summer beverage is a favourite in Granada. It is a light and fruity beverage made by combining red wine with lemon soda or lemonade, which is ideal for enjoying on a warm afternoon.

- **Cerveza Alhambra:** The renowned Cervezas Alhambra brewery, which creates a variety of premium beers, is located in Granada. The Alhambra beers come in a variety of flavours to suit diverse palates, from lagers to artisan brews.

- **Calicasas:** Made in the area, this liqueur is created by distilling wild cherries and other organic components. It has a sweet and fruity flavour and is frequently used in cocktails or as a digestif.

- **Granada-area wine:** The area surrounding Granada is well-known for its vineyards and top-notch wines. The regional wines, which range from crisp whites to strong reds, reflect the distinctive terroir of the region and are the ideal complement to the complex tastes of Granada's cuisine.

An experience in and of itself is Granada's gastronomic scene exploration. The flavours of Granada will stay with you, from special cuisine that reflects the city's cultural legacy to wonderful drinks that quench your thirst. So, when visiting this culinary wonderland, make sure to take advantage of the chance to taste these traditional foods and beverages.

Best Restaurants and Bars in Granada

A variety of restaurants and pubs in Granada cater to a variety of tastes and inclinations, making the city home to a thriving culinary scene. Here are some of the top restaurants in Granada that are renowned for their top-notch fare, appealing atmosphere, and friendly service:

- The restaurant Ruta del Azafrán is a typical Andalusian eatery with a contemporary twist that is situated in the centre of Granada. Their menu offers a variety of dishes produced with products gathered locally, displaying regional flavours and cooking customs.

  Restaurante Ruta del Azafrán is a fantastic option for a special dining experience because of its welcoming ambiance and excellent service.

- **Restaurante Chikito:** Visit Restaurante Chikito for a wonderful dining experience. This well-known restaurant has been providing exquisite Spanish cuisine for many years and has established itself as a Granada culinary landmark.

  The food at Chiquito is a feast for the senses, featuring everything from sumptuous meats to delicious seafood dishes. It is the perfect option for a special event because of its elegant setting and excellent service.

- **Bar Los Diamantes:** If you like tapas, you must go to Bar Los Diamantes. The top tapas in Granada have long been available at this famous bar. The idea is straightforward: order a drink and take advantage of a free tapa of your choice. The tapas at Los Diamantes are a real treat, featuring everything from delectable jamón to freshly fried seafood. The lively ambiance and busy crowd enhance the appeal of this well-liked location.

- **Restaurante Damasqueros:** Located in the district of Albaicin, Restaurante Damasqueros provides a distinctive dining experience with breathtaking views of the Alhambra.

The items on the menu mix classic Spanish flavours with cutting-edge cooking methods to create stunning presentations that are as appetising to the eye as they are to the mouth. Damasqueros is a great option for a special occasion because of its romantic ambiance and superb cuisine.

- **Bodegas Castaneda:** Visit Bodegas Castaneda for a taste of Granada's thriving bar culture. Both residents and tourists alike enjoy dining at this classic pub. The bar serves a wide range of delectable tapas along with a large selection of wines, sherries, and regional beers.

  Bodegas Castaneda is the ideal place to unwind and savour the tastes of Granada because of the lively ambiance, welcoming service, and authentic ambiance.

- La Tana is a tiny wine bar with an excellent range of both domestic and foreign wines that are tucked away in the Albaicin area. A variety of gourmet cheeses, cured meats, and other mouthwatering snacks are also available, and the educated staff can help you navigate their large wine list. La

Tana is a secret treasure for wine connoisseurs because of its modest setting and careful attention to detail.

These are only a few illustrations of the outstanding eateries and pubs in Granada. The city's culinary culture is broad and continuously changing, with new eateries opening up all the time. Granada has a lot to offer food and drink lovers, whether they are looking for gourmet dining, traditional tapas, or a laid-back bar experience.

Tapas Culture in Granada

Granada is distinguished from other Spanish cities by its distinctive and thriving tapas culture. In Granada, you frequently receive a complimentary tapa, a little plate of food, along with your drink when you order a drink at a bar or restaurant. Due to this long-standing custom, food and drink lovers frequently travel to Granada.

The tapas culture of Granada is interwoven in the social fabric of the city and has taken on the status of a way of life for both residents and tourists. It's a beloved tradition that promotes getting together with loved ones, sharing food, and having a good time. Tapas are a sociable and welcome experience since the idea behind them is based on conviviality.

The generous quantities are one of the hallmarks of tapas in Granada. In contrast to other locations where tapas are frequently bite-sized, Granada's portions can be fairly large. You can anticipate a plate full of delectable food, ranging from traditional options like patatas bravas and the Spanish omelette (tortilla espanola) to more sophisticated meals that highlight regional tastes and ingredients.

The variety and diversity of selections are what make Granada's tapas so appealing. Each bar or restaurant has its unique specialties, and you may go on a "tapeo," or tapas crawl, to visit various places and try their food. This enables you to sample a variety of tastes and gourmet delights in a single evening.

Granada's tapas culture goes beyond the country's typical Spanish cuisine. The region's Moorish legacy may be found in the influences, which have led to a combination of flavours and ingredients. For instance, you might come across dishes with Middle Eastern spices or flavours with a Moroccan influence, which adds another level to the tapas experience.

Granada's tapas culture is prevalent across the entire city. Excellent tapas taverns and eateries may be found in a variety of areas, including the city centre, Albaicin, and Realejo. You can learn about many facets of the city's food scene because each region has its own charm and atmosphere.

A few traditions should be remembered when partaking in Granada's tapas culture. It is traditional to place your drink order first, and the bartender or chef will usually decide which tapa to serve. It's usually great to gently express any dietary limitations or preferences you may have. Additionally, don't be hesitant to approach the staff for advice or recommendations; they are often more than pleased to help you choose from the available tapas.

Discovering Granada's tapas culture is a necessity, whether you're a culinary connoisseur or just searching for a genuine and fun dining experience. It's a chance to experience the city's flavours, immerse oneself in its social scene, and make enduring memories. So raise a glass, enjoy some tasty snacks, and experience the tapas culture that makes Granada such a culinary haven.

Market Visits and Cooking Classes

For foodies, visiting the local markets and taking cooking classes in Granada are two of the most satisfying experiences. These experiences provide you the chance to get acquainted with the local culinary customs, find fresh ingredients, and learn to make traditional meals while being guided by accomplished chefs. What to anticipate from Granada's markets and cookery workshops is as follows:

- **Visits to Markets:** Granada is home to a number of bustling markets where you can experience the energetic atmosphere, talk to local merchants, and find a variety of fresh fruits, vegetables, meats, cheeses, and other delectables.

  The Mercado de San Agustin, which lies in the heart of the city, is the most well-known market in

Granada. You may browse the stalls, take in the vibrant fruit and vegetable displays, sample local cheeses and cured meats, and even buy supplies for your own culinary adventures here. The market tour offers an opportunity to interact with the community and offers insight into the regional food culture.

- **Cooking classes:** Learning about the customary methods, tastes, and recipes of Andalusian cuisine is a great way to spend time in Granada. In Granada, there are a lot of culinary schools and organisations that provide lessons for people of all skill levels, from novices to seasoned chefs.

These courses frequently begin with a trip to the neighbourhood market, where you can choose fresh ingredients for your meals.

Then, under the direction of knowledgeable chefs, you'll discover how to make a variety of traditional foods including paella, gazpacho, tapas, or regional delicacies. You may chop, stir, and season your way to a wonderful dinner in the sessions because they frequently stress hands-on participation.

At the conclusion of the session, you'll have the chance to relish the results of your effort and eat the meals you've made, frequently with local wines or snacks.

Market visits and cooking classes have advantages:

- **Cultural Immersion:** Granada's gastronomic traditions and customs can be experienced firsthand through market trips and cooking workshops, which immerse you in the region's food culture.

- **Hands-On Learning:** By participating in these activities, you can learn new cooking techniques, get a better understanding of the flavours and ingredients used in classic dishes, and develop useful skills you can use in your own kitchen.

- **Interaction with Locals:** Attending markets gives you the chance to talk to local sellers, discover their products, and even trade cooking advice and ideas. You'll interact with trained chefs or teachers who can impart their knowledge and expertise when you take cooking classes.

- Cooking class participants frequently leave with recipe cards or booklets, allowing them to reproduce the recipes at home and introduce their loved ones to the flavours of Granada.

- **Social Experience:** Market tours and cooking courses are frequently experienced with other attendees, fostering a social setting where you may meet other foodies, swap tales, and share a love of cooking and cuisine.

Market excursions and cooking lessons in Granada provide a singular chance to learn more about the regional food scene, advance your culinary abilities, and develop a greater understanding of the flavours and traditions of Andalusian cuisine. So get ready to roll up your sleeves, go on a market excursion, and prepare to treat your palate to the genuine flavours of Granada.

OUTDOOR ACTIVITIES AND DAY TRIPS

With its breathtaking natural scenery and advantageous position, Granada provides a wide selection of outdoor activities and day trips for outdoor enthusiasts and thrill seekers. When considering outdoor activities in and around Granada, these are some of the best choices to take into account:

- **Sierra Nevada National Park** is one of the most well-known locations in the area and provides stunning mountain views and outdoor activities all year long.

  On the slopes of the Sierra Nevada Mountains in the winter, you may go skiing and snowboarding. With a variety of routes and vantage points to explore, the park transforms into a refuge for hikers, mountain bikers, and nature enthusiasts during the warmer months.

- **The Alpujarra region**, located south of Granada, is renowned for its charming white-washed villages tucked away in the mountains. Exploring the historic Moorish architecture and culture of the villages, as well as trekking and riding horses, are all excellent activities available in this region. The most lovely villages to visit are Pampaneira, Bubión, and Capileira.

- **Los Cahorros Gorge** is a stunning natural wonder that is ideal for outdoor enthusiasts, and it is close to the town of Monachil and only a short drive from Granada. There are hiking paths in the area that meander through constricting canyons, across hanging bridges, and next to glittering waterfalls. The hike offers a thrilling and all-encompassing experience in nature, and the landscape is spectacular.

- If you're searching for a day excursion that focuses on aquatic sports, think about going to Embalse de los Bermejales. This reservoir provides options for swimming, kayaking, paddleboarding, and fishing. It is bordered by lovely hills and pine forests. It's the perfect place to unwind, soak up the sun, and engage in water-related activities.

- **Cumbres Verdes** is a natural park that provides a tranquil setting for outdoor activities. It is located in the neighbouring municipality of La Zubia. There are many activities to take advantage of the park's breathtaking scenery and clean air, from hiking and mountain biking to picnicking and birdwatching.

- **Salobrena:** Visit Salobrena, a lovely town on the Costa Tropical, for a day trip along the coast. Salobrena provides breathtaking vistas, lovely beaches, and a fascinating old town to discover with its whitewashed homes located on a hillside overlooking the Mediterranean Sea. You may unwind on the beach, savour delicious seafood, or stroll through the winding alleyways while taking in the coastal environment.

These are just a handful of the day trips and outdoor activities that may be done in and around Granada. The area has something to offer everyone, whether they are looking for tranquil hikes, heart-pounding activities, or gorgeous drives. So get ready to enjoy Granada's natural beauty and make lifelong memories amid its alluring surroundings.

Hiking in the Sierra Nevada

Outdoor enthusiasts visiting Granada frequently go hiking in the Sierra Nevada. With their spectacular peaks and varied landscapes, the Sierra Nevada Mountains provide a wide variety of hiking trails that are suitable for hikers of all experience levels and interests.

The following are some significant elements of hiking in the Sierra Nevada:

- **Mulhacén**: Mulhacén, the highest peak in mainland Spain at 3,482 metres (11,423 ft), is a popular hiking destination. For seasoned hikers, reaching the top demands stamina and the right gear, but the stunning views of the surrounding mountains and valleys make the effort worthwhile.

- **Veleta:** At 3,396 metres (11,142 feet) above sea level, Veleta is the second-highest summit in the Sierra Nevada and is another strenuous trek with breathtaking panoramas.

  The Sierra Nevada Ski Resort offers access to the Veleta trail, where hikers can enjoy dramatic scenery and the accomplishment of climbing a lofty peak.

- **Alcazaba:** Alcazaba is a mountain that resembles a fortress that is 3,371 metres (11,060 feet) above sea level. Adventurers who hike to Alcazaba are rewarded with breathtaking views of the nearby peaks and valleys. The trail to Alcazaba is suitable for experienced hikers because it frequently involves navigating rocky terrain and demands good physical fitness.

- **Sulayr GR-240:** The Sulayr GR-240 is a circular trail that circles the Sierra Nevada for about 300 kilometres (186 miles), making it suitable for those looking for longer multi-day hikes.

  Rugged mountains, verdant valleys, and charming villages are just a few of the varied landscapes that the trail offers. Because it is segmented, hikers can pick the parts that best suit their preferences and skill levels.

- Los Cahorros Gorge is traversed on the well-known hiking trail Cahorros de Monachil, which is close to Granada. Hanging bridges, wooden walkways, and cascading waterfalls are all along the trail. It is a favourite destination for hikers and nature lovers due to the unusual rock formations and the lush vegetation that together create a magical atmosphere.

- The La Vereda de la Estrella trail offers breathtaking views and the opportunity to spot local wildlife as it winds through the heart of the Sierra Nevada.

The path takes you through high-altitude landscapes, including mountain passes and pristine valleys, before starting in the charming village of Capileira. It is a strenuous but worthwhile hike that displays the area's natural beauty.

- It is crucial to be well-prepared before starting a hiking adventure in the Sierra Nevada. Make sure to check weather conditions, carry appropriate hiking gear, bring plenty of water and snacks, and have a map or GPS device for navigation. It's also advisable to inform someone of your hiking plans and estimated return time.

Hiking in the Sierra Nevada allows you to immerse yourself in nature, breathe in the fresh mountain air, and wonder at the awe-inspiring views. Whether you're seeking a hard trek to a summit or a leisurely stroll through gorgeous paths, the Sierra Nevada offers an unforgettable hiking experience for all nature aficionados.

Skiing in the Sierra Nevada

A thrilling and well-liked winter activity, skiing in the Sierra Nevada draws tourists from all over the world. The Sierra Nevada offers the best skiing because of its great snow conditions, breathtaking mountain landscape, and well-equipped ski resort. What you should know about skiing in this stunning mountain range is as follows:

- **Sierra Nevada Ski Resort:** Granada residents and visitors may readily access the Sierra Nevada Ski Resort because it is nearby. Skiers of all skill levels can enjoy the incredible variety of ski slopes and amenities that it offers.

  The resort provides a range of amenities, such as accommodations, ski schools, and equipment rentals.

- **Ski Runs and Trails:** The Sierra Nevada Ski Resort offers more than 100 kilometres (62 miles) of ski runs with a variety of challenges for novice, intermediate, and advanced skiers.

  The slopes are well-kept and offer accommodations for cross-country skiing, snowboarding, and alpine skiing. For more daring skiers looking for a challenge, the resort also provides freestyle parks and off-piste zones.

- **Snow Conditions:** The Sierra Nevada has exceptional snow conditions throughout the winter thanks to its high elevation and favourable weather patterns. The ski resort's regular ski season, which runs from late November to early May, provides plenty of chances to ski and snowboard. The area's bright environment also guarantees that there will be plenty of clear days to enjoy the slopes.

- The Sierra Nevada Ski Resort offers a variety of facilities and amenities to improve the skiing experience. Modern ski lifts and gondolas are available, minimising wait times and extending time on the slopes.

  The resort also offers a choice of dining establishments, coffee shops, and après-ski locations where you can unwind, refuel, and take in the lively ambiance.

- **Ski Schools and Lessons:** The Sierra Nevada Ski Resort offers ski schools and lessons for all ages and skill levels, whether you're a novice or trying to advance your abilities. You can receive advanced coaching from qualified instructors or basic instruction from them, which will guarantee a secure and fun day on the slopes.

- **Other Winter sports:** The Sierra Nevada offers a variety of winter sports in addition to skiing and snowboarding. The resort's ice rink is where you may go ice skating, snowshoeing, or tobogganing. Additionally, you may enjoy the majesty of the Sierra Nevada from many angles thanks to the nearby chances for winter trekking, snowmobiling, and even paragliding.

It's crucial to verify the weather and snow conditions before travelling to the Sierra Nevada to go skiing. Booking lodging and ski passes in advance is also a good idea, especially during busy seasons.

It is thrilling and memorable to go skiing in the Sierra Nevada. It is a top destination for lovers of winter sports because of the spectacular mountain scenery, great snow conditions, and well-developed amenities. Grab your skis or snowboard and head out to the slopes to experience the thrill of skiing in this stunning mountain range.

BEACHES NEAR GRANADA

Granada is situated in the interior of Spain, although it is nevertheless close to some of the country's most picturesque coastline regions. Here are a few beaches you can visit in the area of Granada for a day trip or a tranquil beach vacation:

- **Costa Tropical:** To the south of Granada, the Costa Tropical is renowned for its scenic beaches and agreeable weather. Playa de la Herradura, Playa de Almuñécar, and Playa de Salobrena are a few of the well-known beaches in this area.

  These beaches feature beautiful sands, crystal-clear waters, and a variety of facilities like beach bars, eateries, and water sports.

- **Playa de Poniente, Motril:** Playa de Poniente is a long, sandy beach with a wide promenade lined with stores, bars, and restaurants. It is located in the town of Motril. The beach is a great location for a day of sunbathing and relaxation because it has amenities including beach umbrellas, sun loungers, and seaside cafes.

- **Playa de Calahonda:** This picturesque beach, which is close to the municipality of Calahonda, is distinguished by its serene ambiance and crystal-clear waves. Because of its relative seclusion, the beach is a great option for those looking for a relaxing and uncrowded beach experience.

- **Playa de la Rijana:** This undiscovered beach on the Costa Tropical is located in the Cerro

Gordo-La Rijana natural region. This quiet beach has breathtaking views of the Mediterranean Sea and is flanked by cliffs. A short walk is required to get to the beach, contributing to the impression of seclusion and natural beauty.

- Playa de Cantarriján is a charming nudist beach tucked away in a protected cove and is close to the community of La Herradura. The beach is renowned for its stunning surroundings and seas that are crystal pure. There are also eateries by the shore where you may savour local specialties and fresh fish.

- **Playa de Velilla** is a well-liked beach in the town of Almuécar that is renowned for its expansive sandbar and serene seas. Several amenities are available at the beach, including beach bars, places to rent sun loungers, and water sports facilities.

Although these beaches are not located in Granada itself, they are close by and easily accessible by car or public transportation. These coastal regions near Granada offer a variety of options for beach lovers, whether they are looking for a tranquil retreat, water sports activities, or a lively beach atmosphere.

Day trips to nearby cities and towns

Even though Granada is a fascinating city with a lot to discover, several adjacent cities and villages are ideal for day visits. The following are some ideas for day trips from Granada:

- **The city of Cordoba,** which is about two hours drive from Granada, is well-known for its extensive history and stunning architectural marvels. The Mezquita, a magnificent mosque-cathedral that displays a fusion of Islamic and Christian traditions, is the city's main attraction.

  Visit the Alcázar de los Reyes Cristianos, stroll through the lovely grounds of the Alcazar, and explore the quaint alleyways of the Jewish Quarter.

- **Malaga** is a bustling coastal city with a combination of cultural attractions and beautiful beaches that are located on the Costa del Sol. Explore the Alcazaba citadel, go to the Picasso Museum, wander down La Malagueta's bustling promenade, and eat great seafood at the renowned Atarazanas Market. Malaga is also a starting point for trips to the charming cities of Nerja and Marbella.

- **Malaga:** A gorgeous town renowned for its breathtaking views and ancient charm, Ronda is perched atop dramatic cliffs in the Serrania de Ronda Mountains.

Visit the Arab Baths, see the majestic Puente Nuevo bridge that spans a deep gorge, and meander through the Old Town's winding lanes. Try some of the regional wines while you're there because Ronda is known for its wineries.

- **Alpujarra Region:** The Alpujarra region is a lovely area studded with white-washed villages tucked away in the mountains, situated south of Granada. Some of the most charming villages to visit are Pampaneira, Bubión, and Capileira. Enjoy a stroll through their winding alleyways as you take in the historic buildings and the tranquillity of the highlands.

- **Salobrena:** Granada is only a short drive away from this quaint seaside town, which is located on the Costa Tropical. Its picture-perfect whitewashed cottages tumble down a hill and toward the sea. Explore the old town's narrow streets, take a trip to the hilltop Moorish castle, and unwind on the sandy beaches.

- **Guadix:** Known for its distinctive cave dwellings, Guadix provides an intriguing window into an outlandish way of life. Wander through the old streets, take in the stunning Guadix Cathedral, and explore the cave homes. Don't forget to sample the local specialty "Plato alpujarreo," a filling dish made with ingredients from the area.

These are merely a few of the numerous day-trip possibilities offered by Granada. You can explore various facets of Andalusia's rich cultural and natural heritage by visiting any of the destinations because each one has its special charm and attractions to offer. These day trips will enrich and diversify your time in Granada, whether you decide to visit ancient cities, laze on the coast, or climb mountains.

ACCOMMODATIONS

You can choose from a variety of lodging options in Granada to suit your interests and financial situation. Granada boasts a variety of lodging options, including elegant hotels, beautiful boutique hotels, inexpensive hostels, and comfortable guesthouses. Here are some of the city's most well-liked lodging options:

- **Hotels:** Granada is home to a wide range of hotels, from luxurious properties to more reasonably priced alternatives. Numerous hotels are conveniently situated in the city's core, close to the city's top amenities and attractions.

  Internationally recognized hotel chains, boutique hotels with distinctive personalities, and traditional lodging options are all available.

- **Bed & breakfasts and guesthouses:** If you're looking for a more private setting, think about staying at a bed and breakfast or guesthouse. These lodgings offer comfortable rooms with a homey ambiance and are frequently owned by families. Some inns are housed in old structures, making for a pleasant and genuine experience.

- **Hostels:** There are many hostels in Granada, a well-liked destination for backpackers and low-cost vacationers. Both private rooms and dormitory-style rooms at hostels are reasonably priced. They are a fantastic choice for people who want to socialise and meet other travellers. Additionally, a lot of hostels include common areas, kitchens, and planned activities.

- **Apartment rentals:** For individuals looking for more independence and space, renting an apartment can be a great option. In Granada, there are many different apartment rental possibilities, from studios to bigger flats fit for families or groups. Renting an apartment gives you the freedom to cook your meals and live like a local because you have your own kitchen and living space.

- **Country Accommodations:** If you'd rather have a calmer, more natural experience, think about booking a country hotel outside of the city. These lodging options can include farmhouse conversions, rural inns, and country hotels. They offer a chance to unwind in a tranquil setting while still being close to Granada's attractions.

Consider things like location, amenities, and reviews from prior visitors while selecting lodging in Granada. Due to their proximity to popular attractions, travellers frequently choose to stay in the city's heart or the Albayzin district. Additionally, a lot of lodgings provide extras like free Wi-Fi, breakfast choices, and on-site dining.

It is advised to reserve your chosen hotels in advance, especially during the busiest travel times. Websites and online reservation services can offer comprehensive details, images, and reviews to aid in your decision-making.

Overall, Granada has a wide variety of lodging options to meet any visitor's demands, ensuring a relaxing and delightful stay in this energetic city.

Best Places to Stay

Granada's greatest neighbourhoods to stay in depending on your interests and the reason for your trip. Here are some well-liked locations that provide distinctive encounters and easy access to the city's attractions:

- **Albayzin:** A lovely district that offers a window into Granada's past, Albayzin is known for its twisting, serpentine lanes and Moorish influence. When you stay in Albayzin, you may be close to famous sites like the Alhambra and take in breathtaking city views from the Mirador de San Nicolas.

  A variety of lodging options are available in the region, including boutique hotels, guesthouses, and old-fashioned Spanish-style homes.

- **City Center (Centro):** The city centre is a thriving neighbourhood with a lively ambiance, bustling streets, and a variety of stores, eateries, and bars. You can reach popular sites like the Cathedral of Granada, the Royal Chapel, and the busy Plaza Nueva on foot if you stay in the city centre.

  There are several different types of lodging available, including hotels, guesthouses, and flats.

- **Realejo:** Realejo, a historic district with a bohemian vibe, is situated halfway between the city's core and the Alhambra. There are both historic and contemporary attractions available there, such as hip bars, attractive squares, and art galleries. The Alhambra and the city centre are both easily accessible from Realejo, where you can stay. A variety of lodging alternatives are available, from boutique hotels to more affordable inns.

- **The Ronda District** is a residential neighbourhood with a local vibe and is located to the west of the city centre. It provides a calmer setting and a window into Granada's daily life. The city centre is easily accessible by foot from the region, which also offers a good range of eateries and retail establishments. Hotels, inns, and rental apartments are available in the Ronda District.

- **Sacromonte** is a distinctive area in Granada that is well-known for its ancient caverns and flamenco performances. It provides an opportunity to explore the traditional gypsy culture in a bohemian setting. When you stay at Sacromonte, you can take in genuine flamenco performances, tour the cave dwellings, and enjoy sweeping city views. From cave hotels to guesthouses, this region offers a variety of lodging options.

Consider variables like proximity to attractions, your preferred atmosphere, and the kind of experience you're looking for when deciding where in Granada to stay.

Each of these neighbourhoods provides a unique charm and easy access to the city's top attractions. Granada has a neighbourhood to meet your preferences, whether you're looking for historic monuments, a buzzing ambiance, or a peaceful getaway.

Budget-friendly options

There are several options available in Granada if you're searching for inexpensive lodgings that don't sacrifice comfort. Here are some choices that are affordable to think about:

- **Hostels:** Many hostels in Granada are suitable for tourists on a budget. Hostels are a great option for individuals looking for inexpensive housing because they offer dormitory-style quarters with shared amenities.

  For people who prefer more privacy, several hostels also have private rooms. Oasis Backpackers Hostel, Makuto Backpackers Hostel, and White Nest Hostel are a few of the well-known hostels in Granada.

- **Guesthouses and Pensiones:** Guesthouses and pensions are inexpensive lodging options that provide simple amenities and a more individualised experience. These smaller businesses are frequently owned by families and offer nice accommodations at reasonable prices.

  They might not have many conveniences, but they create a warm and inviting atmosphere. The Casa Montalbán Apartamentos, Hostal Lima, and Pension Olympia are a few suggested inns and pensions in Granada.

- **Hotels with a low price tag:** Granada is home to several hotels with a low price tag but offers pleasant lodging. Smaller rooms may be available at some hotels, but they nevertheless offer necessities like Wi-Fi, private toilets, and occasionally even breakfast. The Hotel Anacapri, Hotel Comfort Dauro 2, and Hotel Maciá Monasterio de los Basilios are a few of the less expensive hotel choices in Granada.

- **Apartment rentals:** Renting an apartment can be a budget-friendly choice, particularly for extended periods or for groups of people travelling together. Apartments usually have a kitchenette or a full kitchen, so you may prepare your food and save money. You may find economical options in Granada on several apartment rental websites and platforms, including Airbnb and Booking.com.

- **Off-Peak Seasons and Last-Minute Deals:** Keep an eye out for any last-minute discounts and special offers that hotels and other lodgings may be running. Off-peak times and booking close to your travel dates will yield lower costs. This might be a fantastic option to book inexpensive lodging in Granada.

To get the greatest rates and availability for inexpensive rooms, remember to make your reservations in advance, especially during the busiest travel times. Additionally, think about how close the hotel is to the sights you want to see and whether or not there are public transit options nearby.

By selecting these inexpensive lodging options, you can maximise your trip to Granada without breaking the bank, enabling you to direct your money toward taking advantage of the city's sights, dining, and other activities.

Mid-range Options

There are several choices if you're looking for mid-range lodgings in Granada that strike a balance between comfort and cost. While still inexpensive, these accommodations offer a higher standard of amenities and services. Here are some mid-range choices to take into account:

- **Mid-Range Hotels:** Many mid-range hotels in Granada provide cosy rooms, practical locations, and a variety of amenities. These hotels frequently have on-site dining options, round-the-clock reception services, and other amenities like swimming pools or fitness centres.

  The Hotel Granada Center, Hotel Carmen Granada, and Hotel Comfort Dauro 2 are a few suggested mid-priced lodgings in Granada.

- **Boutique hotels:** There are several attractive and distinctive boutique hotels in Granada. These hotels provide individualised service and pay close attention to detail and are frequently housed in historical structures.

  Granada's boutique hotels combine contemporary conveniences with authentic charm. Gar-Anat Hotel Boutique, Palacio de Santa Ines, and Casa Morisca are a few well-known boutique hotels in Granada.

- **Apartment Hotels:** An apartment hotel combines the luxuries of an apartment with the convenience of a hotel. For families or individuals who prefer self-catering, these lodgings provide roomy rooms or suites with kitchenettes or full kitchens. Additional services like daily housekeeping and concierge help are frequently provided by apartment hotels. Apartamentos Turisticos Alhambra, Apartamentos Taifas, or Abades Nevada Palace are good options for accommodations.

- **Guesthouses and B&Bs:** Granada boasts a choice of mid-range guesthouses and bed and breakfast places that offer a comfortable and welcoming ambiance.

These accommodations are frequently smaller in scale and provide individual service. They may have attractive common rooms, gardens, or rooftop terraces for guests to enjoy. Some recommended guesthouses and

B&Bs in Granada are Casa Bombo, El Ladrón de Agua, and Gar Anat Hotel Boutique.

- **Apart-hotels:** Apart-hotels provide a blend of hotel services and apartment-style lodgings. These accommodations provide completely furnished apartments with separate sleeping and living quarters, making them appropriate for extended visits or for individuals who prefer more independence and space.

  Apartamentos Turisticos San Matas, Aparthotel Abililla, and Apartamentos Montesclaros are a few possibilities to take into consideration.

- To be sure the mid-range accommodations you choose will match your unique needs, take into account things like location, amenities, and guest ratings. To guarantee the greatest prices and availability, it is advised to make reservations in advance, especially during the busiest travel times.

You can have a relaxing and enjoyable stay in Granada with these mid-range lodging options without going over your budget.

Luxury Accommodations

Several high-end lodging options in Granada offer first-rate amenities, first-rate service, and exquisite surroundings for those looking for a lavish and indulgent experience. Here are a few opulent places to stay in Granada:

- **The Parador de Granada** is a renowned hotel with magnificent views of the Alhambra Palace. It is situated on the grounds of the palace. The Parador de Granada is a historic structure that combines Spanish and Moorish architectural styles to create an opulent and exquisite ambiance.

- **The Hotel Alhambra Palace** provides opulent rooms and suites with beautiful views of Granada and the Sierra Nevada mountains. The hotel is perched on a hill above the city. The hotel has a renowned restaurant and terrace in addition to traditional elegance and modern conveniences.

- **Hospes Palacio de los Patos:** This luxurious hotel is housed in a magnificently renovated 19th-century palace that skillfully combines old-world beauty with cutting-edge style. The Hospes Palacio de los Patos offers upscale accommodations, a spa, an outdoor pool, and a fine dining establishment.

- The magnificent hotel, named Eurostars Washington Irving after the well-known American author who wrote about the Alhambra, offers opulent rooms and suites with a dash of refinement. It has a restaurant, a spa, and stunning gardens and is situated in a peaceful area close to the Alhambra.

- The boutique hotel Hotel Villa Oniria is housed in a 19th-century manor house and is conveniently located in the centre of Granada. The Hotel Villa Oniria provides large, tastefully furnished rooms, a spa, an outdoor swimming pool, and a rooftop terrace with expansive city views.

- **Hotel Santa Isabel La Real** is a wonderful boutique hotel with a lovely courtyard, tasteful accommodations, and attentive service. It is situated in the Albayzin area. While still near popular sites, Hotel Santa Isabel La Real offers a peaceful getaway.

- **AC Palacio de Santa Paula:** Situated in a 16th-century monastery, this luxury hotel mixes historical characteristics with modern conveniences. The AC Palacio de Santa Paula offers magnificent accommodations, a spa, a fitness centre, and a restaurant in a tranquil and beautiful environment.

These five-star hotels in Granada offer a high degree of comfort, elegant decor, and first-rate service. They frequently have excellent positions with easy access to the main sights in Granada. Making bookings in advance is advised to guarantee availability, especially during periods of high travel demand.

By selecting one of these opulent lodgings, you can improve your trip to Granada and have a genuinely special and opulent experience.

PRACTICAL INFORMATION

It's crucial to have some useful information when organising your trip to Granada to guarantee a hassle-free and delightful experience. To remember, bear the following information in mind:

- Spanish is the official language of Granada and throughout the rest of Spain. Although English is often spoken in tourist areas, hotels, and some restaurants, knowing a few fundamental Spanish phrases is always useful.

- The Euro (€) is the currency in use in Granada. For smaller businesses that might not accept credit cards, it's a good idea to keep some cash on hand. There are many ATMs scattered throughout the city for easy cash conversion.

- The Central European Time (CET) zone, which is UTC+1, is observed in Granada. The time is advanced to UTC+2 during daylight saving time (late March to late October).

- Citizens of the European Union (EU) or the Schengen Area do not need visas to enter Granada if they have a valid passport or national identity card. The United States, Canada, Australia, and New Zealand are just a few of the nations whose citizens are permitted visa-free entry into Spain as tourists for up to 90 days.

  Before departing, it's best to confirm the precise visa requirements for your place of residency.

- **Transportation**: The city of Granada has a good transportation network. The closest airport, which is about 15 kilometres west of the city, is Granada-Jaen Airport (GRX). You can take a shuttle bus or a taxi to get to the city centre from the airport. Additionally, Granada has a train station and is reachable by bus from other significant Spanish cities.

- Public transportation in Granada is provided by buses that go around the city and its surroundings. The bus system is a cheap and practical means of transportation. Tickets can be purchased at authorised ticket machines or directly from the bus driver. Additionally, taxis are accessible all across the city.

- A Mediterranean climate characterises Granada, with hot summers and moderate winters.

It's crucial to stay hydrated during the summer because it can get quite hot, with temperatures rising above 30 degrees Celsius (86 degrees Fahrenheit). The average winter temperature is between 10 and 15 degrees Celsius (50 and 59 degrees Fahrenheit).

- Travellers can feel safe in Granada in general. But it's always crucial to use common sense care, like watching over your belongings, especially in crowded places and at tourist attractions. You can access emergency assistance by dialling 112.

- **Electricity**: The standard voltage and frequency in Granada are 230 volts and 50 Hz, respectively. The majority of power outlets have two round pins, therefore if your devices have various plug types, you could need a plug converter.

- The majority of Granada's hotels, cafes, and restaurants have free Wi-Fi connectivity. If you need to access the internet or make international calls, you may also locate internet cafés all across the city.

You may more effectively plan for your trip to Granada and make the most of your stay there by keeping these useful suggestions in mind.

Money and Tipping

Here are some crucial things to keep in mind regarding money and tipping in Granada:

- The Euro (€) is the unit of exchange in Granada and the rest of Spain. If you plan to visit any local businesses that might not take credit cards, it is a good idea to have some cash on hand. There are several ATMs scattered throughout the city, making cash withdrawals simple.

- **Credit Cards:** The majority of Granada's hotels, eateries, and businesses accept credit cards. The most widely used credit and debit cards are Visa and Mastercard, but it's a good idea to have some cash on hand as a backup, especially for smaller purchases or in more remote locations.

- **Tipping**: In general, Granada's tipping practices are comparable to those of the rest of Spain. Although it is not required, it is traditional to leave a little tip as a sign of gratitude for excellent service. Here are some tips to remember when tipping:

- **Restaurants**: Depending on the quality of the service, it is customary to leave a tip in the range of 5–10% of the entire bill in restaurants. If the service fee is already included in the bill, tipping is not required.

- **Cafes and Bars**: Tipping is not required at cafes and bars, however, it is customary to round up the bill or leave some spare change as a token of appreciation. You can choose to give a significantly bigger tip if you had an especially good experience or received great treatment.

- **Taxis**: Tipping is not customary in Granada, however as a kindness, you might round up the fare to the closest Euro. You can round up the fare to €9, for instance, if it is €8.50.

- Other **Services**: Tipping is optional for other services such as those provided by hotel personnel, tour guides, or hairstylists. If you are happy with the service, it is traditional to offer a little tip as a sign of thanks. Depending on the quality of the service and your discretion, the amount may change.

Please keep in mind that tips are optional and that the amounts listed above are only suggestions. You can always decide to tip extra generously if you had a particularly memorable encounter or great treatment.

It's also significant to remember that a fee known as "el servicio" is frequently added to restaurant bills in Granada. This amount, which is often a modest portion of the overall payment to cover the cost of service, is not a tip.

In general, tipping is valued and a means to express your gratitude for good service in Granada, even though it is not as prevalent or expected as in some other nations.

LANGUAGE AND COMMUNICATION

Here are some critical things to take into account when it comes to language and communication in Granada:

- Spanish is the official language of Granada and throughout the rest of Spain. In the city, Spanish is commonly spoken and understood.

- **English Proficiency:** Although English isn't as frequently spoken as Spanish, you'll find that many people in Granada, especially those working in the tourism business, have some knowledge of the language. Most major tourist attractions, hotels, restaurants, and tourist hotspots have English-speaking staff on hand to help you with basic communication.

- Learning a few fundamental Spanish words will significantly improve your time in Granada. Locals appreciate the effort, which can facilitate conversations. Greetings (hola, hello, gracias, thank you), fundamental locational questions (Dónde está...?, Where is...?), and standard terms for placing food and beverage orders are a few useful expressions to learn.

- Consider taking a small phrasebook or downloading a language-learning software to your phone that can assist you with translations and pronunciation. When you come into circumstances where English might not be a common language, these tools can come in handy.

- **Non-Verbal Communication**: Gestures and non-verbal clues can also be used to communicate. Keep in mind to be courteous, make eye contact, and respect others' personal space. Even if there is a language barrier, these nonverbal cues can still help you get your point across.

- **Language Exchange**: Granada provides options for language exchange if you're interested in learning more Spanish or honing your language abilities. Many cultural or language schools host language exchange activities where you can meet locals who are eager to practise their English while aiding you in your practice of Spanish.

- **Translation Services**: In circumstances where you need

more thorough translation assistance, Granada offers translation services. These are handy for formal documents, convoluted communication requirements, and emergencies where language support is essential.

Keep in mind that even if you just know a few basic phrases, the people of Granada will appreciate your attempt to speak with them in Spanish. Generally speaking, they are kind and patient, and even if there are some language issues, they will typically try to assist you.

Overall, while it is feasible to go around Granada with little to no Spanish, having a basic command of the language and knowing a few useful phrases will make your trip and interactions with the people much more enjoyable.

USEFUL PHRASES

Here are some essential Spanish expressions you may find helpful while visiting Granada:

Greetings:

Hola - Hello
Buenos días - Good morning
Buenas tardes - Good afternoon
Buenas noches - Good evening/night

Polite Expressions:

Por favor - Please
Gracias - Thank you
De nada - You're welcome
Disculpe - Excuse me

Basic Questions and Directions:

¿Dónde está...? - Where is...?
¿Cómo llego a...? - How do I get to...?
¿Qué hora es? - What time is it?

¿Habla inglés? - Do you speak English?

Ordering Food and Drinks:

Quisiera... - I would like...

La cuenta, por favor - The bill, please

¿Tienes menú en inglés? - Do you have an English menu?

Una cerveza, por favor - One beer, please

Getting Around:

¿Cuánto cuesta el billete? - How much is the ticket?

¿Dónde está la parada de autobús/metro? - Where is the bus/metro stop?

¿Cuánto tiempo tarda en llegar a...? - How long does it take to get to...?

¿A qué hora sale el próximo tren/autobús? - What time does the next train/bus leave?

Emergency Situations:

¡Ayuda! - Help!
¿Dónde está el hospital más cercano? -
Where is the nearest hospital?
Llame a la policía - Call the police
Necesito un médico - I need a doctor

When utilising these expressions, keep
in mind that politeness and respect
should always be shown. Locals will
respect your attempt to speak in their
language, even if your pronunciation is
imperfect.

SAFETY AND HEALTH

When visiting Granada, it is crucial to make sure you are safe and comfortable. Here are some crucial safety and health advice:

Safety precautions in general:

Pay attention to your surroundings and your possessions, especially in crowded places and at tourist attractions.

To safeguard your belongings, use a money belt or a bag with a lock.

Don't flaunt your affluence by wearing pricey jewellery or carrying around a lot of cash.

When using public transit late at night, use dependable services and proceed with caution.

Keep to populated, well-lit locations, especially at night.

Facilities for health and medicine:

Excellent healthcare facilities, including hospitals and clinics, are available in Granada, together with highly qualified medical staff.

Having travel insurance that pays for unexpected medical costs or other situations is advised.

Bring a copy of your travel insurance information and any required medical documentation with you.

Make sure you have plenty of any specific drugs you need for the duration of your trip.

Health precautions and vaccinations:

If any vaccines are advised for your trip to Granada, check with your neighbourhood doctor or travel clinic.

Regular immunizations against measles, mumps, rubella, diphtheria, pertussis, tetanus, and influenza are advised to remain current.

If you intend to visit rural areas, use insect repellent to avoid mosquito bites.
Keep yourself hydrated, especially during the hot summer months, and cover up with sunscreen to avoid skin cancer.
Services for Emergencies:

To contact police, fire, and medical services in an emergency, dial the 112 emergency number in Europe.
Having the phone number for your embassy or consulate in Granada is also a smart idea.

Travel Warnings:

Keep abreast of any travel advice or cautions published by the government of your nation on visits to Granada.

Before your journey, register with your embassy or consulate to obtain any updates or critical information.

It's important to remember that Granada is often a safe city for visitors. You may enjoy this lovely location without stress by taking some simple safety precautions and abiding by local laws and customs.

LOCAL CUSTOMS AND ETIQUETTE

Your cultural experience and interactions with residents in Granada will be enhanced if you are aware of and respect local customs and etiquette. To remember, have the following in mind:

- **Greetings:** It's usual to say "Hola" (hello) or "Buenos días/tardes/noches" (good morning, afternoon, or evening) when you first meet someone or enter a store or restaurant. In official contexts, handshakes are typical, but among friends or in more relaxed settings, a kiss on each cheek or a warm hug may be given.

- **Personal Space:** Compared to certain other cultures, Spanish individuals often value their own privacy and stand a little closer together during conversations. It's crucial to respect others' personal space and to refrain from standing too close as this could come across as chilly or distant.

- **Dining Etiquette:** It is polite to be on time or a few minutes late when invited to someone's home for a meal. Keep your hands on the table rather than on your lap and wait to be seated at all times. It is considerate to sample a bit of everything that is offered and to consume all that is on your plate.

  Additionally, it is customary to thank the host for the lunch. It's customary to stay at the table after a meal when dining out, enjoying conversation and perhaps getting coffee or dessert.

- **Tipping:** Although it has already been mentioned, it is important to note that in Granada, tipping is less common than in some other nations. However, it's customary to leave a little tip as a sign of gratitude for excellent service. Depending on the quality of the service, you can round up the price or leave a tip of between 5 and 10% of the total.

- **Siesta:** The siesta is a customary noon break in Granada, as it is throughout much of Spain. The typical closing time for stores and companies in the afternoon is between 2:00 PM and 5:00 PM. Locals might rest or take a nap during this period. When organising your activities, it's crucial to keep this in mind and to modify your calendar accordingly.

- Although Granada is a rather casual city, it is appropriate to dress modestly when visiting sacred places or upscale restaurants. In such locations, stay away from wearing beachwear or revealing attire. Casual and comfy clothes are typically acceptable in more laid-back environments.

- Courtesy and civility are values that the Spanish people hold dear. When communicating with locals, saying "por favour" (please) and "gracias" (thank you) goes a long way. When speaking to someone you don't know well, it's also normal to use "seor" (sir) or "senora/senorita" (madam/miss), followed by their last name or position.

You will encourage positive encounters and make a good impression on the residents in Granada if you are aware of and respect their traditions and manners. Accept cultural differences and take pleasure in getting to know the locals' way of life.

CONCLUSION

In conclusion, Granada is a fascinating city with a colourful culture, stunning landmarks, and a rich history. You now have a thorough understanding of Granada, allowing you to explore the city's hidden beauties and take advantage of everything it has to offer.

You will immerse yourself in the city's fascinating history and varied architecture as you tour the spectacular Alhambra Palace, the Generalife Gardens, the Cathedral of Granada, and the Albayzin area. Sacromonte Caves and the breathtaking Mirador de San Nicolas both provide fascinating viewpoints and insights into Granada's historic legacy.

You can splurge on regional food and savour the flavours of regional specialties while immersing yourself in the tapas' culture. Additionally, participating in cooking workshops and market excursions will deepen your understanding of regional culinary customs.

The Sierra Nevada offers chances for trekking and skiing, while the close-by beaches offer leisure and coastal exploration. Granada's natural beauty extends beyond the city's boundaries.

From inexpensive lodging to opulent hotels that offer a touch of elegance and comfort, Granada offers a variety of lodging alternatives to fit every preference and budget.

Being aware of regional customs and etiquette can help you to respect and appreciate the local culture throughout your trip.

With this travel guide in hand, you are well-equipped to set out on a memorable tour to uncover Granada's hidden gems. Granada welcomes guests with open arms.

Pack your luggage, enjoy this magical city's charm, and let Granada seduce you with its natural splendour, rich history, and gracious people. Enjoy Granada as your ultimate travel destination!

Final Thoughts on Visiting Granada in 2023

There are a few last things to consider as you prepare to travel to Granada in 2023:

- **Check the Travel Limits:** Before your journey, it's crucial to be aware of any limits or guidelines that may have been put in place because of regional or international events. Be aware of any unique rules that may affect your trips to Granada, such as entry restrictions, health precautions, and other regulations.

- Granada is a well-liked tourist destination, particularly during the busiest times of the year. It's a good idea to plan and make the appropriate bookings for lodging, activities, and transportation to make the most of your vacation. A smoother and more enjoyable experience will result from doing this.

- Granada is a city rich in history and tradition, so embrace it. Spend some time getting to know the people, trying the local cuisine, and learning about the customs of the area. Take advantage of the chance to get to know the locals, attend events, and discover the hidden attractions that make Granada special.

- **Be Flexible:** when preparation is crucial, you should also try to be adaptable when you are there. The best memories are frequently the results of unanticipated discoveries and spontaneous events. Give yourself permission to detour from your plan, see off-the-beaten-path areas, and enjoy travelling by chance.

- The beautiful natural scenery and ancient sites in Granada should be respected. Always consider your environmental impact when travelling responsibly. Respect the cultural and natural legacy by abstaining from any actions that might hurt or degrade it by staying on designated trails, appropriately disposing of rubbish, and so on.

- Granada's inhabitants are renowned for their friendliness and kindness. Spend some time interacting with the locals, hearing their stories, and gaining an understanding of their way of life. Connecting with the locals may enhance your travel experience, whether it is over a cup of coffee or by taking part in cultural events.

- **Capture the Moments:** From the breathtaking Alhambra to the quaint alleyways of Albayzin, Granada offers endless photo opportunities. Capture the city's beauty and make enduring memories. But keep in mind to also take some time to see the sights personally and be fully present.

A trip to Granada in 2023 is sure to be a memorable one, rich in history, culture, and scenic beauty. You can make priceless memories and gain a greater understanding of this interesting city by making advance plans, observing local customs, and going into your vacation with an open mind. Have fun on the trip to Granada!

Additional Resources for Planning Your Trip to Granada

To make the most of your vacation, planning a trip to Granada entails gathering knowledge and resources. Here are some other tools to aid in your vacation preparation:

- **Official Tourism Website:** The Granada tourism board's official website is a great place to find out all there is to know about the city, including its attractions, events, lodging options, and useful information. For the most recent information and insights, go to their website at www.turgranada.es.

- **Travel guidebooks:** Granada-specific travel guides can offer in-depth details about the city's history, attractions, and insider tips. Granada is frequently covered in well-known guidebook series like Lonely Planet, Rick Steves, and DK Eyewitness Travel.

- **Online travel forums:** On sites like TripAdvisor and Lonely Planet's Thorn Tree, travellers can find a wealth of knowledge and perspectives from other visitors who have been to Granada. You can get advice, suggestions, and solutions to particular travel-related queries.

- **Travel websites and blogs:** Many travel websites and blogs give their own experiences as well as advice for travelling to Granada. Look for trustworthy travel blogs or websites that concentrate on Spain or Granada in particular, as they frequently include thorough itineraries, restaurant choices, and off-the-beaten-path ideas.

- Local guidebooks and maps are available at bookstores, gift shops, and tourist information offices after you arrive in Granada. These sources frequently include detailed information on lesser-known attractions, walking routes, and neighbourhood hints.

- **Social media:** On websites like Instagram, Twitter, and Facebook, search for Granada-related hashtags and official tourist accounts. You'll have access to up-to-date information, stunning images, and advice from residents and other tourists.

- **Local Celebrations:** Granada offers several celebrations all through the year, from religious processions to musical and cultural events. To discover if any events coincide with the dates of your trip, check the local calendars of events or go to the tourism board's website.

To ensure accuracy and up-to-date information, keep in mind to cross-reference data from several sources. Making use of these tools will improve your trip preparation and give you important insights into maximising your time in Granada.